NATURAL LEADERSHIP DEVELOPMENT

MᶜKINLEY JOHNSON

① little foxes spoil The vine.
② God knows my heart and helps
every step y The way.

CREATION
HOUSE
A STRANG COMPANY

NATURAL LEADERSHIP DEVELOPMENT by McKinley Johnson
Published by Creation House
A Strang Company
600 Rinehart Road
Lake Mary, Florida 32746
www.creationhouse.com

This book or parts thereof may not be reproduced in any form, stored in a retrieval system, or transmitted in any form by any means—electronic, mechanical, photocopy, recording, or otherwise—without prior written permission of the publisher, except as provided by United States of America copyright law.

Unless otherwise noted, all Scripture quotations are from the Holy Bible, New International Version. Copyright © 1973, 1978, 1984, International Bible Society. Used by permission.

Scripture quotations marked NKJV are from the New King James Version of the Bible. Copyright © 1979, 1980, 1982 by Thomas Nelson, Inc., publishers. Used by permission.

Cover design by Terry Clifton

Copyright © 2006 by McKinley Johnson
All rights reserved

Library of Congress Control Number: 2006923955

International Standard Book Number: 1-59979-014-9

First Edition

06 07 08 09 10 — 987654321
Printed in the United States of America

This book is dedicated to the following people:

- To Jesus Christ, my Savior, Lord, and King, whose wisdom, council, and might have enabled me to accomplish more than I could ever ask for. Thank You.

- To my mother, Rutha Mae Johnson, whose unconditional love and support have empowered me to achieve extraordinary results.

- To my father, Otha Dean Johnson, Sr., whose discipline and hard work modeled the essence of true success.

- To you, the reader, whose leadership causes you to see, think, and act strategically in order to respond to ever-changing needs.

ACKNOWLEDGMENTS

I WOULD LIKE TO give a special thanks to my professor, mentor, and friend, Dr. Jacque King, Regent University, The School of Leadership Studies, whose constant support and direction has helped me to accomplish my dream.

Also, I would like to thank Sarah Cron for proofreading and editing my book, making it both well written and reader friendly.

In addition, I want to thank everyone who has played a significant role in my life and leadership. This book is the product of your wisdom and council, which has been poured into me throughout the years.

To all my family, your love and support means a great deal to me.

To my brother Bobby Johnson, Sr., thank you for believing in me.

CONTENTS

PREFACE

With the rise and fall of so many leaders in recent years, many people are asking difficult questions about the nature, character, and authority of leaders. All these questions can be answered with a grass roots understanding of leadership.

After spending more than eighteen years in the accounting profession, ten years in church leadership, and several years pursuing various graduate degrees in leadership studies, experience has taught this author the importance of understanding how God uses the leader's environment as a tool to enhance individual and organizational effectiveness. This book offers a unique biblical perspective for understanding the leader and the environment and the impact both can have on each other for the furtherance of the kingdom of God.

INTRODUCTION

Natural leadership development is a collaborative partnership between God, humanity, and the environment. This joint venture is built on goodwill and trust and is critically important for achieving optimum success. In the wake of profound economic, social, and political unrest, the Bible offers an innovative strategic model for leaders of organizations to use as a guide for reshaping their skills and redefining their companies during difficult times.

Understanding natural leadership development can help companies stay ahead of the leadership gap that many of them are experiencing. It can also reduce stress and anxiety while it increases overall satisfaction. Leadership satisfaction was an integral part of God's strategic planning process from the beginning, and it is one reason He charged humanity to take dominion and authority over the earth.

However, since the fall of humanity the need for leaders to reduce stress and anxiety through fair strategies and structures has become increasingly necessary. To create a fair and equitable base for everyone, the leaders must devise plans that fit within the political, social, cultural, economic, educational, and religious structures of the day. Responding correctly to these rapidly changing environments requires courage, imagination, and mental agility.

Natural leadership development focuses on what the Bible teaches about the process of leadership. Although the Bible does not use the term *natural leadership development* it does show that there is a natural development to leadership. The underlying principles of this process are universal in nature and are beneficial to those who seek a biblical understanding of the environmental influences that shape leaders.

This is not a naturalistic perspective devoid of God. The term *natural* is used because it proclaims God as the Creator. Scripture tells us who God is and what He requires of leaders. Nature shows God's deeds in creation and testifies that He is intimately involved in human affairs.

There are five significant keys to understanding natural leadership development:

1. **Deep-seated desire**—Inherent within each person is a deeply rooted desire to become the leader God intended. Without a drive to discover our leadership potential, we will fail to satisfy God's purpose for our lives.

2. **God's design**—God's purpose in creating man and woman was to fill the earth and subdue it.

3. **Right relationships**—Leadership works best when leaders live in harmony with God and each other. God's original intent was for men to live in harmony with one another.

4. **Stewardship**—Leaders are responsible for managing.

5. **God's creation**—We must give earnest heed to how
   we use our resources, gifts, talents, and abilities, so
   we can give a good account of our leadership.

Leaders who develop naturally seek to serve the interest of others rather than their own interest. The apostle Paul's admonition to the Philippians is instructive: "Each of you should look not only to your own interest, but also to the interest of others" (Phil. 2:4).

The term *natural* means "according to nature." In other words, *natural* could also be taken to mean "God-initiated." If we take our cues from nature, we will learn from God, the greatest teacher of all. But defining *leadership* is not as simple as defining nature. Leadership varies in terms of behaviors, influences, relationships, and purposes.

In his book *Leadership in Organizations*, Gary Yukl defines leadership as "the ability of an individual to influence, motivate, and enable others to contribute toward the effectiveness and success of the organization."[1] Influence is the common theme in every variation of the definition of leadership.

The same is true in natural leadership development. However, in the early stages of this process leaders receive influence from outside sources. An understanding of the relational dynamics between the environment and the leader is required for a full understanding of natural leadership development. Therefore, natural leadership development can best be defined as the process of understanding the environmental influences that shape the nature, character, and authority of leaders.

The seed of leadership is sown in the heart of every person. However, a leader must be placed in the right environment for this seed to germinate properly. Not all environments are conducive to natural leadership development. Personal experiences can either ignite or retard this development. But when you are placed in the right circumstances and respond positively to those influences, you will become the great leader you were created to be.

In natural leadership development, God initiates the process by placing a potential leader in the right environment. This includes your family of origin, the place where you grew up, and your life experiences. These are all significant in God's overall plan.

A person who has stood against the winds of adversity is a great leader in the making. To maximize leadership potential, the environment must contain the necessary ingredients to produce the fruits of leadership. Without the proper ingredients of spirituality, societal interaction, and cultural influences, a person's ability to lead will be reduced to mediocrity. To avoid this pitfall, it is important to grasp the process of natural leadership development at the beginning and at the completion of a person's leadership journey.

Your reach extends far beyond the scope of your vision, mission, and purpose. Your work is never really finished, but lives on in the lives of those you have influenced. Just as a vine has many branches, a leader influences many followers who will eventually become leaders themselves. A final integral part of natural leadership development is the passing of the leadership mantle. The legacy of a great leader is not found in the mere achieving of individual or organizational goals; it is, however, birthed in your ability to pass the fruits of your knowledge, skills, and experience to the next generation of leaders.

BIBLICAL ROOTS OF NATURAL
LEADERSHIP DEVELOPMENT

As I stated in the introduction, natural leadership development can best be defined as the process of understanding the environmental influences that shape the nature, character, and authority of leaders. This concept is not expressly identified in the Bible, but it is deeply rooted there. A careful examination of Genesis, chapters 1 and 2, reveals the following: (a) God created man from the dust of the earth—*nature*, (b) man was made in the image of God—*character*, and (c) man was given dominion by God to rule over the earth—*authority*.

The creation account shows that Adam and Eve were placed in a perfect situation—a flawless environment—with the nature, character, and authority of leadership. The development of this leadership is a process that happens in the following distinct areas: (a) The leader's relationship with the Creator, (b) the leader's relationship with others, and (c) the leader's relationship with the environment.

The Creation of Man—Nature

Many of the leadership problems that face our political, social, cultural, educational, religious, and economic structures can be resolved by paying close attention to the Word of God. The Creation account implies that the environment plays a significant role in a person's development. Therefore, it is imperative to take a closer look at the biblical text and discover the underlying patterns and principles at work in this environment.

Have you ever wondered why you have the parents you do? Why did you grow up in a certain city and go to a particular school? Why did you experience the things that happened in your early life? Our circumstances do not happen by chance. Each person has a greater purpose that can only be fulfilled by being placed in the specific environment that God has designed for them. In the Creation account, God began by creating the perfect environment that would develop Adam and Eve's natural leadership abilities.

Although numerous leadership programs are available and even helpful, the environment provides all the natural ingredients needed to help you reach your highest potential. The environment is an integral part of God's overall strategic plan for your development. Similarities may exist, but no environment is exactly identical.

For Adam and Eve to reach their full leadership potential, God had to plant them in the right environment—the ideal situation. The same is true of every generation. The environment determines the leader's potential. Without the right circumstances, a leader's growth and development will be stunted. The right environment is filled with endless possibilities, new opportunities, and tremendous challenges specifically designed to build character and maximize potential.

OVERCOMING OBSTACLES
THAT STUNT PERSONAL GROWTH

Four major obstacles will stunt a Christian leader's growth: (1) A lack of focus, (2) a refusal to take action, (3) an unwillingness to manage leadership progress, and (4) a lack of tenacity. In contrast, since the majority of natural leadership development will actually happen in the environment, you must do four key things to maximize your leadership development. First, you must recognize and appreciate the situation for all it is worth. You must not grow bitter about the environment in which God has planted you, but instead choose to grow stronger and wiser by using your difficulties to sharpen your leadership skills.

Second, you must develop a network of support to help facilitate changes that arise from various challenges. No person can do it alone. Third, you should develop the right mental attitude. Attitude determines the breadth and depth of a person's leadership potential. A negative attitude will stunt natural leadership development. Finally, you must be willing to modify your leadership style to match the situation; no one style fits all.

You can do many things to maximize your development as a leader. Ultimately, however, disobedience to God's commands is the biggest obstacle to growth. The story of Jonah illustrates what happens when an emerging leader is reluctant to obey God's commands. Even if Jonah thought he could run from his leadership lesson by refusing to go to Nineveh (Jon. 1:3), his disobedience did not change God's purposes for his development. God remained committed to Jonah's growth even if it meant preparing a great fish to help him, and His commitment to us is the same.

Reluctant Jonah finally obeyed God and accomplished His gracious purposes by facing the challenges to his leadership. However, he missed a great opportunity to grow as a leader.

Jonah failed to realize that God was just as interested in saving him as a leader as He was in saving the Ninevites as a people.

As a leader you should not run from leadership challenges or shirk responsibilities because of difficulties or dissatisfaction. Instead, you must be willing to learn from them. If you remain focused, take decisive action when necessary, manage your leadership progress, and endure in the face of adversity, you are overcoming obstacles that would limit your leadership development.

Remembering the mnemonic F.A.M.E. can help you avoid the four major obstacles to growth:

F = Focus
A = Action
M = Manage
E = Endure

Likewise, applying the principles of F.A.M.E. can help you achieve your goals. F.A.M.E. requires staying *focused* on the stated objective, taking decisive *action* toward the objective, *managing* the progress, and *enduring* until the goal is reached.

The parable of the talents in Matthew 25:14–30 is a great example of how the principles of this mnemonic device are used as a leadership tool to accomplish God's purposes on earth. In this parable, a leader took a trip to a faraway country. Just before he left, he entrusted three of his followers with various levels of leadership responsibilities, based on their natural talents, gifts, and abilities. To one he gave five talents, to another two talents, and to another one talent. The leader instructed his followers to use their abilities to grow the business until he returned.

When he returned, the leader called a meeting for an update on their progress. As they sat around the boardroom table, the followers gave their reports. The one with five talents had gained five more by being focused, taking decisive actions, managing his progress, and enduring until he reached his goal. The follower who had been given two talents told how he had used his skills to gain two additional talents. But the third individual who had been given only one talent made excuses for not using his abilities to increase the business.

The leader congratulated the two followers who used their natural leadership tools to increase the business. However, he gave the unprofitable follower a stern rebuke, took the only talent he had been given, and gave it to the one who had profited the most. Ultimately, followers and emerging leaders who refuse to exercise their natural leadership abilities are unprofitable to the organization and to the kingdom of God. The fruit of successful leadership is productivity.

MEASURING SUCCESSFUL LEADERSHIP

From a biblical perspective, successful leadership is determined by three variables: faith, commitment, and healthy (right) relationships. Without these, it is impossible to accomplish anything. In essence, the degree of success is determined by the investment. The level of success is equal to the level of the leader's faith and commitment to healthy relationships.

To observe these three variables in action, it is necessary to once again consider the Creator and His creation. Creation demonstrates that God's highest purpose for natural leadership is relationships. Healthy relationships are comprised of five essential building blocks: respect, trust, support, honesty, and accountability.

Building healthy relationships is really a way of life that begins with the heart. At the heart of good leadership is a respect for other people and their cultures, a belief in the potential of others, and an understanding that beliefs and values guide both decisions and actions. In addition, good leaders recognize the difference between covenants and contracts;

personal relationships count for more than formal structures and systems.[1]

It takes time to build good relationships. However, if a leader is skilled in the art of developing healthy relationships, the result will be well worth the investment. God invested quality time in cultivating His relationship with Adam. The result was that Adam also invested quality time in cultivating his relationship with Eve and their children. Since God invested so much of His leadership values and principles into humanity, He entrusted His creation into our care. This teaches another key leadership principle: leaders who express confidence in others send a clear message that says, "I value our relationship."

THE IMAGE OF GOD—CHARACTER

For help in examining the relationship between God and humanity, we consider Genesis 1:26–27:

> Then God said, "Let us make man in our image, in our likeness, and let them rule over the fish of the sea and the birds of the air, over the livestock, over all the earth, and over all the creatures that move along the ground." So God created man in his own image, in the image of God he created him; male and female he created them.

Genesis 1 provides a revelation of the image of God and His likeness in humanity. The following verses paint a poignant word picture of this:

1. Genesis 1:1 (emphasis added)—"In the beginning God *created* the heavens and the earth."

2. Genesis 1:3—"And God said...and there was light."

3. Genesis 1:6–7—"And God said...And it was so."

4. Genesis 1:9—"And God said...And it was so."

5. Genesis 1:11—"Then God said... And it was so."

6. Genesis 1:14–15—"And God said... And it was so."

7. Genesis 1:20–21—"And God said... And God saw that it was good."

8. Genesis 1:24—"And God said... And it was so."

The *image of God* demonstrates God as the Creator and Sustainer of all creation. When God speaks in Genesis 1, the Spirit brings that spoken word into reality. He reveals Himself in both word and deed. If our character is to reflect the *image of God*, our words must have corresponding actions.

This is crucial to understanding natural leadership development. Self-identity comes from God. If you do not know who God is, then you will never discover who you are in Him. In fact, because you are made in the image and likeness of God, He is the only mirror that accurately reflects who you are as a spirit-being.

If the character of God is revealed in both word and deed, so is the character of humanity. The creative force behind our words goes before us to prepare the reality of our spoken words. That which is spoken will eventually happen. Like the bit in a horse's mouth or the rudder on a ship, the leader controls the organization (James 3:1–12).

But what controls the leader? James says the tongue does— your spoken words that represent your thoughts and ideas. This is affirmed in *The Leadership Bible: Leadership Principles From God's Word*: "What a leader says has great power to affect an organization—either for better or for worse."[2]

AN ENVIRONMENT FOR GROWTH

The environment God created for Adam and Eve was filled with endless possibilities, new opportunities, and tremendous challenges. The Garden of Eden had everything Adam, Eve, and every other generation needed to develop their nature, character, and authority. It was the ideal situation for developing core leadership competencies, which, according to *Going Virtual*, are the products of three ingredients: (1) Knowledge, (2) acquired skill, and (3) experience.[3] Adam and Eve were taught by the best and were given enough information to make informed decisions, overcome obstacles, and meet the growing demands of all creation.

God schooled Adam and Eve by planting them in a creative environment to explore the wonders of its glory. The Garden of Eden was characterized by its freedom and openness, two key ingredients that foster support and encourage creativity. The only command they received was this: "You are free to eat from any tree in the garden; but you must not eat from the tree of the knowledge of good and evil, for when you eat of it you will surely die" (Gen. 2:16–17).

If God had initially laid down a list of rules and regulations and reprimanded Adam and Eve for thinking outside of the box, the garden would have stifled their natural leadership growth. Instead, God created an atmosphere of creativity by making it an integral part of the garden's design. Adam and Eve had creativity in their DNA, but the situation in which they were placed enhanced that ability.

UNLOCKING CREATIVITY
IN THE ENVIRONMENT

Many may think that their environment is chaotic and a hindrance to growth, and it is therefore constructive to create what is known as "positive turbulence."[4] This involves the development of creative climates where innovation and renewal can take place. One of the common threads among geniuses like Einstein, Edison, da Vinci, and Mozart is that they were able to see things slightly different than the norm.

The ability to see, think, and act differently is critical for surviving any environment, especially today.

Positive turbulence is necessary for unlocking creativity in an environment. God created the perfect environment for Adam and Eve to challenge them to reflect His image in them. The image of God was best reflected when Adam and Eve were united in spirit and purpose, working together to subdue and rule over the work of God's creation (Gen. 1:28).

The Creation account of Genesis 2 emphasizes the covenant relationship between Adam and Eve. The unity between them was designed to express the harmony of the triune existence of God the Father, God the Son, and God the Holy Spirit. The key to a quality relationship with others is a right relationship with God. A healthy relationship with others will determine if you can use chaotic energy and direct it toward positive outcomes.

Although Adam and Eve were physically different, they were able to harness their differences to complement each other and meet God's stated goals and objectives for them. The same is true for leading an organization through chaos, complexity, and change into rich fulfillment. Differences between individuals do not imply deficiencies; they are a vital part of God's overall strategy for natural leadership development.

Because of the uniqueness of their environment, Adam and Eve were forced to find creative ways to work together to satisfy the needs of creation. If the first generation was able to work together to resolve issues, how much more should the generations of the twenty-first century be able to use our cultural, ethnic, political, social, economic, educational, and religious backgrounds to address today's concerns for the good of humanity.

EXERCISING DOMINION—AUTHORITY

The life of Jesus demonstrates that leaders will be able to overcome adversity and exercise their God-given authority when they

13

cultivate and maintain a right relationship with God. Although God does not always save us from difficulties, He often saves us through difficulties. A close look at Jesus' life in Luke 2:39–52 illustrates God's natural leadership development process.

When Joseph and Mary had performed everything the Law required for the birth of Jesus, they returned to Nazareth. Jesus grew up in Nazareth, became strong in spirit and wisdom, and gained favor with God and man. According to custom, Joseph took his family to Jerusalem every year to celebrate the Feast of the Passover.

However, when Jesus was twelve years old, He stayed behind after the feast ended, and everyone returned to their respective cities. When Mary and Joseph realized that their son was not in their company of people, they turned back to Jerusalem to look for him. After three days, they finally found Him in the temple, sitting among the religious leaders, listening and asking questions.

Although the leaders were amazed at His understanding, Mary and Joseph were astounded that He would do this to them:

> His mother said to him, "Son, why have you treated us like this? Your father and I have been anxiously searching for you." "Why were you searching for me?" he asked. "Didn't you know I had to be in my Father's house?" But they did not understand what he was saying to them.
>
> —LUKE 2:48–50

Jesus' question demonstrated that He understood leadership authority to be God-initiated. He could have believed God's timing for His Messianic anointing was at hand. But even if Jesus understood God's purpose for His life at an early age, He was not ready to walk in it. And although Mary and Joseph did not understand what their son meant by His statement, Jesus humbled Himself and returned with them to Nazareth.

He continued to grow in stature and wisdom, working and

studying for eighteen years until God was ready for Him to assume His Messianic purpose. By age thirty, Jesus was finally ready to fulfill all righteousness. Consider Luke's description of Jesus' baptism:

> When all the people were being baptized, Jesus was baptized too. And as he was praying, heaven was opened and the Holy Spirit descended on him in bodily form like a dove. And a voice came from heaven: "You are my Son; whom I love; with you I am well pleased."
>
> —LUKE 3:21–22

This scene is very different from His earlier pre-launch at age twelve, and it reveals a key principle: when leaders follow God's ordained plan, His presence will affirm and confirm their leadership decisions. How well you live according to God's Word is a sure way to determine if you are ready for the reins of leadership.

Before Jesus could walk in the full measure of His authority, He had to walk through the wilderness. He could not circumvent God's process even though He had all wisdom and understanding. After forty days in the wilderness, Jesus returned in the power of the Holy Spirit, demonstrating His authority over forces that held men and women captive.

One of the most challenging forces many leaders face today is the feeling of utter hopelessness among their followers. With all the changes in society, the rise and fall of the economy, and the increase in sickness and diseases, many people cannot help but feel insecure. Jesus used His God-given authority to address these needs in His day. He healed the sick, raised the dead, and fed the multitudes. There was no lack when Jesus was around, and this teaches another principle: when leaders walk in the full measure of their calling, every need around them will be satisfied. This is no ordinary life.

Everything Jesus said and did was based on what He heard

the Father say and what He saw the Father doing (John 5:19; 8:26–30). His attitude, conversation, conduct, and behavior mirrored His Father's. Notice the candid conversation Jesus had with His disciples about His nature, character, and authority:

> The words I say to you are not just my own. Rather, it is the Father, living in me, who is doing his work. Believe me when I say that I am in the Father and the Father is in me...
>
> —JOHN 14:10–11

Likewise, as a Christian leader, everything you say and do must mirror the words and actions of your Savior, Lord, and King. Just as Christ was one with His Father, you must be one with Christ if you are to walk in the fullness of your calling. Only humility, which is the balance of authority, will make this possible. The apostle Paul summed up the authority of Jesus in the following manner:

> Who, being in very nature God, did not consider equality with God something to be grasped, but made himself nothing, taking the very nature of a servant, being made in human likeness. And being found in appearance as a man, he humbled himself and became obedient to death—even death on a cross!
>
> —PHILIPPIANS 2:6–8

The main goal for leaders is to reflect the humility of Christ while they exercise His authority. Christ's love is the bond that unites leaders and followers, and the environment requires Christlikeness from everyone. Leaders must follow God's Word and be empowered by the indwelling Holy Spirit if they are to use their God-given authority properly and meet the growing demands of the environment.

GOD-INITIATED LEADERSHIP

T HE BIBLICAL NARRATIVE reveals a glimpse of the creation of man and woman, who together reflect the image of God. Genesis 2:7 tells how God was intimately involved in this process. "The LORD God formed the man from the dust of the ground and breathed into his nostrils the breath of life, and the man became a living being."

The author of Genesis takes great care to describe God's meticulous design of man. God did not just throw man together like pieces of a puzzle. Instead, He took dust, and fashioned man in His image and likeness, from the crown of his head to the soles of his feet.

After creating the skeletal and molecular structure, God brought man face-to-face with Him, breathed into his nostrils, and made man a living being. Man was endowed with all the attributes of the Creator to operate in the earth as He commanded. "So God created man in his own image, in the image of God he created him; male and female he created them" (Gen. 1:27).

GOD'S DESIGN AND NATURAL LEADERSHIP DEVELOPMENT

The Creation account shows that God designed the concept of natural leadership development when He placed man in the Garden of Eden and instructed them to take care of it. God's next order of business was to help man assume their natural leadership role. Notice how God initiated, orchestrated, and superintended this process:

> Now the LORD God had formed out of the ground all the beasts of the field and all the birds of the air. He brought them to the man to see what he would name them; and whatever the man called each living creature, that was its name. So the man gave names to all the livestock, the birds of the air and all the beasts of the field.
>
> —GENESIS 2:19–20

The natural leadership development process began when God brought the animals to Adam to see what he would do. God never told Adam to name the animals; He wanted him to take the initiative. This event defined Adam's leadership over creation as God originally intended. God knew that man, given the right context, would assume the reins of leadership.

Natural leadership development empowers people through preparatory education to reach their natural leadership potential. When Adam was given the opportunity, he asserted his leadership in a manner that pleased the Creator. God affirmed Adam's leadership behavior, as the author of Genesis showed with the statement, "Whatever the man called each living creature, that was its name" (Gen. 2:19).

THE FALL OF HUMANITY

Because of the complex, diverse, and ambiguous nature of the rational environment, Adam and Eve needed to maintain a healthy relationship with God to accomplish the tasks entrusted to them (Gen. 2:8–15). Healthy attitudes, beliefs, and values proceed out of an intimate relationship with God. Without an intimate relationship with the Creator, Adam and Eve's leadership would have collapsed under the weightiness of God's awesome creation. In fact, this is what happened.

The door to all sorts of evil opened up when Adam and Eve disobeyed God's command (Gen. 2:16–17; 3:14–19). In direct violation of God's command not to eat from the tree of the knowledge of good and evil, Eve and her husband, Adam, chose knowledge and human attainment over obedience to God. Their choice to pursue knowledge and human attainment has been repeated many times throughout history. A recent example—the 2001 Enron corporate scandal—is discussed below, and it illustrates what happens when leaders do not follow God's principles in the execution of their responsibilities.

Understanding the fundamental principles of natural leadership development enables leaders to see beyond ratios, goals, and bottom lines. Great leaders realize that they are dependent upon God's strength and guidance. God's leadership provided Adam and Eve with a sense of meaning, fulfillment, and purpose. He provided Adam and Eve with a rational environment that strengthened their values, built trust, infused human dignity, and promoted opportunities for personal growth. Likewise, good leaders free others to be their best as God did with His creation.

Building a close relationship with God requires close attention to His Word. Through the Word, leaders discover that respect, trust, support, honesty, and accountability are fundamental elements of success. Any leader who practices these values will reap the benefits of leadership health. Obedience to the Word of God gives distinction and expression to deeply held beliefs. It acts as the driving force behind great leadership.

THE COLLAPSE OF A GREAT CORPORATION

The 2001 Enron scandal demonstrates the disastrous results that unprincipled leadership can produce. With the enormous complexities revealed through the media and court transcripts, it may take many years to fully understand the root cause of Enron's fall.[1] Nonetheless, the jury found the leadership of Enron responsible for deceptive practices and bilking people out of billions of dollars.

Enron's illegalities are important because of the scale and scope of the corporation's leadership failures. The Enron scandal and others like it had a devastating effect on the economy at the very time the nation was mourning the losses of the terrorist attacks on September 11, 2001. However, focusing only on the criminal activity misses the most critical point. Enron is in ruins today because of deceptive leadership practices prompted by personal greed.

The apostle Paul forewarned Timothy of the effects poor decision-making can have on an organization whose sole ambition is personal gain:

> People who want to get rich fall into temptation and a trap and into many foolish and harmful desires that plunge men into ruin and destruction. For the love of money is a root of all kinds of evil. Some people, eager for money, have wandered from the faith and pierced themselves with many griefs.
>
> —1 TIMOTHY 6:9–10

Paul's warning reminds leaders that self-centeredness, if it is left unattended, will lead to corruption. The misalignment of individual and biblical values leads to self-centeredness and other destructive tendencies. Enron's leadership should have realized that values exist because they give a needed sense of right and wrong, good and bad.

Milton Rokeach, an early scholar of human morals, defined

values as "enduring beliefs that a specific mode of conduct or end state of existence is personally and/or socially preferable to an opposite or converse mode of conduct or end state of existence" [2] Values give distinction and expression to deeply held beliefs.[3] More important, values reveal who we are, what we are about, what we stand for, and what we will or will not do.[4]

Values are at the core of leadership behavior, and leaders must pay close attention to their personal and organizational values. It is important to note that deeply held beliefs are only as good as their source. For the Christian, a close relationship with God will both inform and keep in check those beliefs that are critical to success. Enron's failure serves as a prime example of what can happen if good values are allowed to slip from the heart.

Joanne Ciulla, in *Ethics: the Heart of Leadership*, suggests that because values are transformational, they will often include others. Good values, then, are by nature "others-centered" and must be worked out in the context of community.[5] Values, therefore, are significant to natural leadership development because of the mutual benefits they offer both leaders and followers.

The benefits of communicating biblical values cannot be overstated. However articulating company values can open a window for the spread of hypocrisy.[6] Again, the examples of Enron and other organizations show that leadership values must not only be communicated to followers, but also modeled by leaders. Hypocrisy occurs when leaders seek to change the behavior of others but do not bother to change their own.

If organizational change is to be achieved, leaders must be the first to make the necessary changes and emulate the desired behavior. To be effective, leaders must communicate the values and norms of the organization through words and corresponding actions. If values and norms are only verbalized, hypocrisy becomes a hidden value.

Hidden values usually lurk behind inconsistent behavior. A periodic values assessment can be beneficial for tracking consistent and inconsistent behavior.[7] For large corporations like Enron, establishing a values auditor (independent or otherwise) who can periodically assess individual and organizational values may prove to be a valuable resource.

Leadership inconsistencies create a stumbling block for followers to achieve the desired values, norms, and behaviors of the organization. In the final analysis, developing consistent behavior over time is the only solution for this. It requires leaders to be disciplined, determined, and tenacious in the face of temptation.

Organizations that minimize or even fail to identify potential blind spots such as greed and deception could fall into ruin. However, Christian leaders can reduce the likelihood of this by paying close attention to the Word of God and to wise counsel.

LESSONS FROM THE TEMPTATION OF CHRIST

Because natural leadership development is God-initiated, leaders must model the spiritual and ethical business practices taught in His Word. Jesus used God's Word to shape His leadership and to guide His decisions when He faced the same temptations leaders face today.

Luke 4:1–13 shows that Jesus wrestled with temptation as Eve did in the Garden of Eden (Gen. 3:1–7). Unlike Eve and her husband, however, Jesus never surrendered or yielded to the lure of Satan's deceit. Sin is not found in temptation itself, but in yielding to it. Luke's narrative gives insight for defeating temptation:

> Jesus, full of the Holy Spirit, returned from the Jordan and was led by the Spirit in the desert, where for forty days he was tempted by the devil. He ate nothing during those days, and at the end of them he was hungry.
> —LUKE 4:1–2

The interior life of the leader is a crucial aspect of natural leadership development. If it is left unattended, it will go unnoticed until the bitter fruit of neglect works its way into other areas of the leader's behavior. Jesus separated Himself for a specific period of time to deal with His inner life, and this is a key lesson for leaders.

One of the surest ways to defeat temptation is to fast and pray through it. The length of time for fasting can be determined by the degree of temptation. Jesus fasted forty days to thwart the relentless temptations of the devil. Jesus also told His disciples to pray without giving up (Luke 18:1). The underlying principle is crucial: the likelihood of a leader yielding to temptation dramatically increases with an undisciplined spirit.

Fasting and praying help to bring undisciplined passions under control. These passions often stunt your natural leadership development, and your followers usually reap the consequences. Therefore, it is vitally important for you to attend to your own soul (i.e., private life) while you juggle everything else (i.e., public life). Failure to do this will result in symptoms that hinder your personal growth and leadership health.

Another key principle in defeating temptation is to disarm it with the Word of God. Again, Luke illustrates how Jesus kept His passions in check:

> The devil said to him, "If you are the Son of God, tell this stone to become bread." Jesus *answered*, "It is written: 'Man does not live on bread alone.'" The devil led him up to a high place and showed him in an instant all the kingdoms of the world. . . . "So if you worship me, it will all be yours." Jesus *answered*, "It is written: 'Worship the Lord your God and serve him only.'" The devil led him to Jerusalem and had him stand on the highest point of the temple. "If you are the Son of God," he said, "throw yourself down from here . . . Jesus *answered*, "It says: 'Do not put the Lord your God to the test.'"
> —LUKE 4:3–12, EMPHASIS ADDED

NATURAL LEADERSHIP DEVELOPMENT

Satan bombarded Jesus' mind with thoughts of position, power, and prestige. He knew that these ambitions could ultimately thwart Christ's mission and message, and he wanted to do to Christ what he had done to Adam and Eve: sever His relationship with the Father and render Him powerless to fulfill the plan of salvation. Every temptation from Satan is designed to subtly move us away from God with growing demands that require increasingly greater sacrifices until all natural leadership authority has been yielded to him.

However, Jesus showed that a sure way to defeat temptation and disarm battles in the mind is to verbalize the Word of God and act accordingly. His example paved the way for leaders today to overcome the lust of the flesh, the lust of the eye, and the pride of life. Christ defeated every temptation by bringing every thought into captivity through the Word of God.

Finally, consider Paul's words of comfort to the Corinthian church:

> No temptation has seized you except what is common to man. And God is faithful; he will not let you be tempted beyond what you can bear. But when you are tempted, he will also provide a way out so that you can stand up under it.
>
> —1 CORINTHIANS 10:13

Paul emphasizes God's faithfulness to make a way of escape so that we do not have to yield to its relentless pressure. A wise leader takes God's escape route.

THE NATURAL LEADERSHIP DEVELOPMENT TEST

Luke teaches another important lesson about the temptation of Jesus. He had to pass the natural leadership development test before He could walk in His Messianic anointing and heal the sick, raise the dead, feed the multitudes, and deliver those oppressed by the devil. And every leader who is called of God must take this test.

Again, Luke 4:1 reveals some key principles: "Jesus, full of the Holy Spirit, returned from the Jordan and was led by the Spirit…" Notice that after Jesus' affirmation and confirmation at the Jordan River, the Holy Spirit led Him to the wilderness to be tested. During this time, Jesus fasts and prays. Fasting and praying neutralize the fleshly mind and allow for a greater focus on God's Word and its application.

Before God can trust a person with true leadership responsibilities, He must see if that person can be trusted. God in His foreknowledge already knows this, but He still requires the exam to test an emerging leader's submission, loyalty, and obedience to Him and His Word. When the children of Israel were taking this test, Moses gave them this instruction:

> Be careful to follow every command I am giving you today, so that you may live and increase and may enter and possess the land that the LORD promised on oath to your forefathers. Remember how the LORD your God led you all the way in the desert these forty years, *to humble you and to test you in order to know what was in your heart, whether or not you would keep his commands.*
> —DEUTERONOMY 8:1–2, EMPHASIS ADDED

The only appropriate response to the grace of God is humble submission, loyalty, and obedience. This is the only way to prove faithfulness to God in the natural leadership development process. There is no way to circumvent the wilderness exam. A leader must pass it before walking in the full measure of the natural leadership calling. It determines if the leader can be trusted with the true riches of God's kingdom.

Although natural leadership development is God-initiated, it does not shield a leader from coming under fire. Sometimes tough trials call a person's faith and commitment into question.

During these difficult times a leader benefits most from drawing closer to God through prayer, fasting, devotions, and fellowship. A leader will face trials, but should not be caught off-guard. The apostle Peter wrote:

> Dear friends, do not be surprised at the painful trial you are suffering, as though something strange were happening to you. But rejoice that you participate in the sufferings of Christ, so that you may be overjoyed when his glory is revealed.
>
> —1 PETER 4:12–13

A truly successful leader follows God's prescribed plan for leadership development, as it is outlined in His Word. However, Scripture and current events reveal the great tragedy that happens when a leader tries to circumvent it. Two critical principles are at work here: first, natural leadership development is an overriding priority for effective leadership. Second, effective leadership is developed over time and must be viewed as a lifelong goal.

God is in the business of cultivating leaders through the environment to satisfy His purposes. Leaders called by God are empowered by the Holy Spirit to use their skills to influence as many people as possible for Him.

THE SEED OF LEADERSHIP
AND ITS HEALING IMPACT

Rᴇᴘʟɪᴄᴀᴛɪᴏɴ ɪꜱ ᴀ key aspect of natural leadership development. God recognized this when He gave this command to
Adam and Eve:

> Be fruitful and increase in number; fill the earth and
> subdue it. Rule over the fish of the sea and the birds of
> the air and over every living creature that moves on the
> ground.
>
> —Gᴇɴᴇꜱɪꜱ 1:28

Although this word was spoken to Adam and Eve it was
sown into the heart of humanity. As people grow and mature
so does the Word that is sown in their hearts. Since God's
Word is both spirit and life, it cannot return to Him without
accomplishing its mission. Notice what God said about the
power of His Word:

As the rain and the snow come down from heaven, and do not return to it without watering the earth and making it bud and flourish, so that it yields seed for the sower and bread for the eater, so is my word that goes out from my mouth: It will not return to me empty, but will accomplish what I desire and achieve the purpose for which I sent it.

—ISAIAH 55:10–11

No matter where God calls you to leadership—in business, church, public service, entertainment, or any other segment of society—your choices will determine the type of leader you become. In other words, leadership is what you make it. However, God will make every attempt to develop successful leaders. His Word is so sure that neither sin nor death will stop this from happening. The fall of man illustrates this.

After the fall, God assured Adam and Eve that the heel of the woman's seed would bruise the head of the serpent (Gen. 3:15). Since then, God has been using people to create specific strategies and structures to facilitate the salvation of humanity. The unfolding of God's plan of salvation is fully realized in the life, ministry, death, and resurrection of Jesus.

God's plan, both before and after Jesus' incarnation, has been to call people from a dying world and show them His grace (Hosea 2:23). The purpose of this gift of grace is to demonstrate God's endless love for humanity. Good leaders will incorporate this truth into their businesses, churches, institutions, and organizations.

This life-changing message of hope must be communicated through our social, political, cultural, and economic systems. God has not given up hope for the salvation of all humanity. He created the ultimate plan of salvation, which was fulfilled through Jesus. Today, Christian leaders are called to create strategies and structures that allow the transcendent presence of God to break into human history and offer this salvation to the world. Organizational strategies and structures play a key role in God's grand scheme. Heaven is God's dwelling place, but He has planned it so that humanity no longer has to reach for the sky. Instead, God reaches down to the earth through organizations, leaders, and followers. God's master plan is designed to move humanity from simply "being together" to actually "living together." [1]

LEADERSHIP THAT CHANGES THE WORLD

The highest purpose of leadership is to build healthy relationships consisting of goodwill and trust. As I stated earlier, healthy relationships are critically important to natural leadership development and are primarily a matter of the heart. At the heart of leadership is a respect for other people and their cultures, a belief in the potential of others, and an understanding that beliefs and values guide both decisions and actions.

It takes time, energy, and emotional investment to build good relationships. They do not just happen, but they are determined largely by the personal and organizational choices you make. In business, you must have an intimate knowledge of your organization and the environment to make good decisions about your products and services. Knowing your own business requires mobilizing company resources in a way that creates the greatest impact for good in the world.

For example, to make good business decisions you must know the following about your company: (a) Its products, (b) the cost of its products, (c) its resource capabilities (i.e., human, capital, and material), and (d) the potential impact all these can have on the market. Knowing the product line, cost structure, resource capabilities, and market potential sets the parameters and direction of an organization.

But mobilizing people and resources requires goodwill and

trust from both inside and outside an organization. Goodwill and trust are the capstone of godly character. Thus, godly character is perhaps the single greatest need of any organization. It is an essential part of natural leadership development. Godly character will encompass these five key values:

1. **Respect**—Respecting and appreciating people of different cultures, backgrounds, and ethnicity are tangible expressions of Christlike character. Only the nature of Christ can give a leader the ability to embrace diversity.

2. **Trust**—Ultimately, leaders bear the responsibility for building trusting relationships. Leaders who trust others are more likely to "share sensitive information, disclose problems, delegate authority, and ask for participation in decision making."[2]

3. **Support**—Leaders should support cross-cultural and sensitivity training as a means to moving beyond awareness to a deep appreciation for diversity.

4. **Honesty**—A leader's earnest conviction will earn respect and loyalty from followers. Honesty is the foundation of trust between leaders and followers. By modeling honesty, a leader minimizes skepticism and builds healthy relationships.[3]

5. **Accountability**—Leadership can also be defined as accountability. One of the driving forces behind a leader's performance and behavior is the ability to respond responsibly to others.

For Christ-centered leaders, these shared values transcend barriers by creating an atmosphere conducive to goodwill and trust. R. Daft's book, *Leadership Theory and Practice*, says, "Emotional connections are risky; however, they are necessary if true leadership is to happen."[4] Putting people first improves the quality of decision-making while it promotes goodwill and trust among leaders and followers. This is the dynamic of a healthy relationship.

Recognizing and establishing healthy relationships are an integral part of natural leadership development and one of the highest purposes of the kingdom of God. Research has proven that people desire healthy relationships and seek to satisfy this need through various means. Social and behavioral theorists such as Abraham Maslow, Douglas McGregor, Frederick Herzberg, and David McClelland have made attempts to explain and predict observable behavior. [5]

These theorists hold a diversity of basic assumptions and beliefs about human nature driven by their respective philosophical and theological perspectives. But these perspectives are significant for understanding human motivation. Philosophers and scholars have theorized for centuries about the internal needs and motives of people only to discover just how complex human nature is.

Despite this, human desire has been commonly categorized into three basic needs: (a) The need for love (1 John 4:7–11), (b) the need for leadership (Ps. 23), and (c) the need for recognition for a job well done (Matt. 25:20–23). These three fundamental needs are sown in the heart of every person and have their roots in Creation. They provide a frame of reference for understanding today's realities.

An understanding of history's purpose further clarifies the process of natural leadership development. History only has meaning if it is moving toward a goal, a fact that is evident throughout Scripture. The theme of promises and their fulfillments is woven throughout the Bible.

Jesus, being the express image of God in the flesh, is the fulfillment of the promise God made in the Garden of Eden (Gen. 3:15). As God's representative on earth, Jesus preached the fundamental message that His kingdom was at hand.

History finds its meaning through the life of Jesus.

Since God through Christ predetermined that history should have a future, it is up to leaders to discern God's plan for this future and work toward that end. Therefore, leading involves complex strategic planning and mobilizing resources to facilitate the needs of humanity. Formulating a good plan requires the following: making calculations, setting priorities, allocating resources, utilizing all available means, and collaborating with other people.

But organizational strategies and structures are not limited to the natural sphere. God's plan of salvation for humanity reaches the spiritual sphere, and this requires careful consideration, reflection, and prayer. Ultimately, the organizational mission is a primary means to bring health and wholeness to the environment and to the world. This plan extends to future generations in every geographical location.

NATURAL LEADERSHIP DEVELOPMENT AND THE FUTURE

If leaders are to bring health and wholeness to the world, they must consider several questions: how much time should leaders spend thinking about the future? How should leaders motivate and encourage others to actively participate in future forecasting? How do leaders do this in a work environment where repetition and productivity are valued above future thinking?

These questions and others like them have significant value not just because they relate to profit margins, but because they relate to time. Most people can readily identify with a lack of time and money. But good leaders, being visionary in nature, seem to suppress the pressures of the fast-paced environment to enjoy the serenity of *futuring*.

Futuring is the process by which future studies are applied to individual and organizational life to better prepare for the future. This involves understanding the long-term forces of change as they affect the planet and people, both the whole of humanity and the individual. At the core, futuring is "trend tracking, scenario development, visioning, strategic planning, and change management." [7]

Ultimately, the only leaders worth following are those with a vision based on God's preferred future. Jesus is a prime example of such a leader. His vision of eternal life compelled people to organize themselves and mobilize their resources for change. Acts 2:44–45 tells how "all the believers were together and had everything in common. Selling their possessions and goods, they gave to anyone as he had need."

Change in Jerusalem and neighboring cities had been long overdue, but there had not been a capable visionary leader until Jesus stepped onto the scene. In Jerusalem, the change He instigated brought people closer together. Consider Acts 2:46–47:

> Every day they continued to meet together in the temple courts. They broke bread in their homes and ate together with glad and sincere hearts, praising God and enjoying the favor of all the people. And the Lord added to their number daily those who were being saved.

Change ushered in an opportunity for the message of Jesus to move into the national spotlight and onto the world stage.

COPING WITH CHANGE

Change, not stability, is the norm for past, present, and future realities. During Christ's lifetime and the time of the early church, change occurred incrementally and infrequently. But in today's environment and economy, change is both dramatic and constant.

Incremental and infrequent changes represent a state of equilibrium in the environment and the economy, whereas dramatic and constant changes are radical for any society. Since the latter type of change is now inevitable, strategic planning must include a vision of the future. G. Ringland says, "In this environment, the techniques used for planning over the past decades are no longer sufficient, and may be misleading... Good planning requires a forward view of the future."[8]

Leaders must adapt and modify their behavior to keep up with the pace of the future. Changes in the environment will determine which strategic plan best fits the situation. But whatever method you choose, you would be wise to first consult God in future planning. Proverbs 3:5–6 states: "Trust in the Lord with all your heart and lean not on your own understanding; in all your ways acknowledge him, and he will make your paths straight."

The intent of natural leadership development is to maintain and improve the quality of life for everyone by focusing on what is *possible* (what can or could be), *probable* (what is likely to be), and *preferable* (what ought to be).[9] Any organization that does not include long-range planning in its strategy will ultimately cease to exist because it failed to see beyond its present state of existence.

Successful strategic planning translates a compelling vision and a strong mission into purposeful actions that best benefit the organization, the individual, and the environment for the long haul. If you are to achieve this desired, preferred future, you must formulate a strategy with specific steps to help your organization attain it.

This principle is clearly evident when Jesus selected twelve disciples and developed them into church leaders to continue the work of the kingdom after He was gone. Christ delegated this ministry to His disciples through the Great Commission in Matthew 28:18–20. He gave His disciples a strategic plan that compelled them to serve Him with their gifts, talents, and natural abilities through the power of the Holy Spirit.

Jesus effectively adapted His leadership activity to the realities of the situation. He instructed His disciples when they were uninformed, directed them when they were confused, prodded them when they were reluctant, and encouraged them when they were downhearted. When they were ready, He gave them limited tasks and responsibilities and then participated with them, guiding them through their assignments. Finally, He empowered and commissioned them as His apostles.[10]

This was the method by which Jesus chose to help His disciples reach their preferred future.

To attain the preferred future, you need to answer three important questions about your organization: (1) Where is the organization now? (2) Where does it want to be in ten or twenty years? (3) What changes does it need to make to get there? Finding good answers to these questions will bring you, your organization, and its members into alignment with its desired goals. Failure to implement the preferred future strategy will ultimately send an organization spiraling downward toward an undesirable future.

THE LEADER AS GOD'S MORAL AGENT

Your impact on the future depends on your ability to deal effectively with the political, social, and cultural influences of the day. But when you encounter these three areas, it is imperative that you keep a proper focus and remember your God-given identity as one of His moral agents on earth. You can accomplish this by infusing biblical values and principles throughout your organization.

Christ intends for today's Christian leaders to influence society just as He did during His earthly ministry. Biblical values and principles lead to a right relationship with Jesus Christ and foster respect, trust, support, honesty, and accountability. Maintaining a clear conscience and a pure heart is the only way to infuse Christ's values and principles into our political, social, and cultural systems. Failure to clearly identify and model acceptable values and norms will open the door to further anomie, chaos, and purposelessness.

Leaders must not forget their primary mission to be God's moral agents on earth. If leaders choose not to deal effectively with their political, social, and cultural environments these societal institutions will eventually stifle the missionary efforts of Christian organizations. Writing in *The Community of the King*, Howard A. Snyder warns leaders that if Christians place more emphasis on social consciousness than on kingdom consciousness, their impact on organizations, leaders, and followers will slip into obscurity.[11]

The obscurity Christian leaders could experience in the future will be directly related to an identity crisis they face. Christian leaders are to be salt and light in the world. According to Jesus, believers "are the salt of the earth. But if the salt loses its saltiness, how can it be made salty again? It is no longer good for anything, except to be thrown out and trampled by men" (Matt. 5:13). It is imperative that Christian leaders maintain their God-given identity and focus on being God's moral agents on earth.

FUTURE LEADERSHIP CRISIS

The potential identity crisis of the future will certainly be the result of the consumer mentality that is so pervasive in our culture. Already, the current cultural values and norms have so captured Christian leaders that they often equate success with size and incorporate the use of marketing strategies and analysis, apart from the counsel of God's Word, to increase growth.

If Christian leaders continue to identify more with the culture than with Christ, they will progressively leave God's original mission—the ministry of reconciliation—and become nothing more than a movement that seeks to captivate the masses with its political and social agendas. While there is nothing wrong with Christian leaders desiring to influence the political and social climate, they must maintain the standards of holiness that Christ taught.

In marketing, the desire for future growth will require that the method and message change according to the targeted segment of society. Consumers will not be interested in what an organization stands for, but in the fulfillment of what it can deliver. However, Christian leaders must stay the course and so must their organizations, businesses, and academic institutions. The real measure of success in the future will be found in the leader's ability to stay on course with the original vision and mission of the organization.

FUTURE STRATEGIES AND STRUCTURES

Conventional wisdom might suggest that a traditional strategy with a top-down hierarchical structure will work best for any organization. However, given today's environmental complexities, competitive climate, technological advancements, markets, and various processes, the traditional approach may cause more harm than good. Typically, when the competitive advantage is greater, the organizational structure must provide greater support for growing demands.

A biblical understanding of organizational structure is radically different from the world's perspective. Initially, biblically based organizations were created and designed to establish and further God's kingdom on earth. Future organizations should continue to follow this beaten path of God's reconciliatory purposes by creating strategies and structures that make provisions for the salvation of humanity. Christ's compelling sacrifice is God's strategic plan for salvation, which biblically based organizations should support.

When the influence of Christ is upon an organization, it

will be an instrument through which the transcendent presence of God can permeate society and offer again His gift of salvation to the world. Future organizational structures will be successful when they translate a compelling vision, a strong mission, and core values into purposeful actions that benefit the entire world.

The way a Christian leader handles uncertainty and tension will determine if Christianity will prove beneficial to organizations as a whole. Since radical changes will continue to happen in technology and in the political and social structures, people will need to become more resourceful to combat uncertainty. The only way for Christian leaders to do this is to become more knowledgeable about the areas of tension. Through the wise use of knowledge, Christian leaders will be able to dispel uncertainty and bring calm to mounting tension.

As organizations look to the future, they will face greater demands to hire highly competent people. The pool of qualified candidates will grow, adding yet another layer of complexity to organizational life. In addition, the competitive nature of the marketplace will press Christian leaders to extend the reach of their organizations by exploring new territories, finding new markets, and forging new relationships.

Despite enormous challenges, godly leaders will have to develop organizations, businesses, and institutions that impact the values and norms of their political, social, and cultural environments. It is essential that leaders be inquisitive about similarities and differences that exist among people, for this will determine their level of influence on society and the world. General curiosity can assist in building bridges that foster healthy relationships. The seed of leadership that determines success in the future will be one that forces organizations, leaders, and followers to look inward, outward, and forward.

RECOGNIZING THE ENVIRONMENT
FOR ALL ITS WORTH

As I mentioned in the introduction, the seed of leadership is sown in the heart of every person. However, the emerging leader must be placed in the right environment for this seed to germinate properly. The environment can be defined as the factors and conditions that influence an individual. It includes your political, social, cultural, economic, educational, and religious background. It is designed to provide you with endless possibilities, new opportunities, and tremendous challenges, and it is the ideal situation for developing core leadership competencies.

MOSES AND HIS ENVIRONMENT

The life of Moses is an example of how God uses the environment to shape the nature, character, and authority of a leader. Widely admired as a Hebrew prophet, leader, and teacher, his legacy shows that God uses ordinary people to do extraordinary things. Moses was born in the land of Egypt, of the tribe of Levi, the son of Amram and Jochebed, and the brother of Aaron and Miriam (Exod. 2:1–2, 6:20; 1 Chron. 6:3). He was born during a very difficult time in Israel's history.

The people of Israel, who had lived in Egypt since the time of Joseph, had increased in number so greatly that the Egyptians began to view them as a national security threat. Pharaoh, the ruler of Egypt, placed the Israelites under a brutal slavery system and also ordered that all male children born to Hebrew slaves be drowned in the Nile River (Exod. 1:6–14, 22).

To escape the ruler's wrathful edict, Jochebed hid Moses for three months. When she could no longer hide him, she put him in a waterproof basket and placed it near the riverbank. Pharaoh's daughter found the child, had compassion on him, and reared him as her own. She named him Moses, which literally translates "drawn out of the water." At the suggestion of his sister Miriam, Pharaoh's daughter hired Jochebed to nurse him until he was weaned (Exod. 2:1–10).

Moses was raised in Pharaoh's house where he was educated in all the wisdom of the Egyptians. At the time, the Egyptians were well-known for their political, social, cultural, economic, educational, and religious systems. This environment provided a freedom and openness that fostered, supported, and encouraged natural leadership development, and God used it to prepare Moses for future leadership.

Egypt was one the wealthiest nations at this time. Historically, wealth produces sophisticated strategies, structures, and systems, and these elements would all play an integral role in Israel's deliverance and establishment as a nation. Also, although Moses was raised in Pharaoh's house, Jochebed instilled in him a knowledge of his heritage and a love for his people. This influence began to grow in him as he saw the slavery and oppression of his people for forty years.

When the Egyptian hatred of Israel became too much for Moses to handle, he killed an Egyptian man and hid him in the sand. He found himself on Egypt's most wanted list and was forced to flee to Midian. There, he married Zipporah, the daughter of a Midianite priest named Jethro, and spent another forty years tending his father-in-law's sheep (Exod. 2:11–21; 3:1). During this time, Moses received training for his future task of shepherding the children of Israel.

When Moses was eighty years old, God appeared to him in a burning bush and gave him his natural leadership development assignment: lead the Israelites out of Egypt. The training he had received in the environments of both Egypt and Midian had prepared him for the greatest challenge to his leadership: spending forty years with the Israelites in the wilderness.

God chose Moses to lead His people out of Egyptian slavery and into the Promised Land. With the help of his brother, Aaron, Moses spoke to Pharaoh several times. The ruler's attitude and behavior brought ten plagues upon his land (Exod. 3–12), and this eventually broke the bonds of slavery. Moses led the Israelites out of the land of Egypt, through the Red Sea, into the wilderness, and just short of the Promised Land.

God showed through many infallible proofs that He was Israel's strong tower, protector, deliverer, provider, and healer. Yet the people of Israel often resisted God's will by turning their problems into their dwelling place. Unfortunately, Israel's greatest testimony slowly became the rod that God used to judge Moses and his generation. But the wilderness experience was more than just a testing ground; it became the birthplace of a new nation.

The wilderness experience gave Moses time to establish the young nation's political, social, religious, and cultural systems. These were designed to minimize conflict, give Israel distinctiveness, and help them achieve God's overall objective for their existence. To accomplish such a great feat, several steps had to be taken.

First, Moses needed a plan to assist Israel in becoming a great nation. Second, he found a way to rally the people around the stated goals and objectives. Third, Moses understood that people need something to believe in and work toward so they could achieve their highest potential. Fourth, he knew that all activities should be structured to fulfill the overall purpose. Finally, to maximize performance, Moses had to manage the work.[1]

Moses brought organizational structure to Israel. The following is a list of some of his most distinguished accomplishments:

1. He received the Ten Commandments from God and gave them to the people to help them relate to God and to one another (Exod. 20:1–17).

2. Under God's directions, he supervised the construction of the tabernacle and the ark of the covenant (Exod. 25–26).

3. He authored the Torah, the first five books of the Bible.

Even with these accomplishments, Moses still wrestled with weakness as any leader will. But like other biblical leaders, he realized that Israel's deliverance was totally dependent on God. His life demonstrates a key biblical principle: dependence on God—not the absence of weakness—makes a leader strong (2 Cor. 12:10).

THE ENVIRONMENT: A TOOL FOR GROWTH

As the previous section shows, God used the environment as a tool for natural leadership development in the life of Moses. Not all environments foster freedom and openness; some stifle or retard this process. For a leader to become the person God has created him to be, he must be placed in the right political, social, cultural, educational, economic, and religious context.

It is important to note that the right environment is not necessarily the best of all environments. It simply provides the best setting for the development of a person's natural leadership abilities. Some people grow best when all odds are against them. Others can grow only when circumstances are favorable. God knows what context or situation is best for a future leader. As He prepared Moses to deliver Israel from slavery, He placed Moses in the right environment.

THE VALUE OF THE ENVIRONMENT

The environment, with its institutional influences, is an integral part of the natural leadership development process. There are essentially two types of environments. One type fosters a freedom and openness necessary for emerging leaders to develop necessary skills and competencies. It encourages them to embrace change through education, training, and personal interaction. A second type helps leaders grow through acquired knowledge, skill, and experiences in both their personal and professional development.

You may be in both types of environments at various times during your life, as Moses was. Any environment, even the most volatile, is conducive to learning. Typically, however, good environments are characterized as settings that promote personal and professional development and provide for improved communication and collaboration through creativity and innovation.

The life of Moses demonstrates that every environment has the capacity to become a natural leadership development tool. Because the environment promotes communication and collaboration, everyone engaged in the process can identify and solve problems together. This gives you room to experiment, improve, and increase your leadership capabilities.[2]

For example, when Moses was leading Israel in the desert, he communicated and collaborated with his father-in-law Jethro.

Based on the advice he received from Jethro (Exod. 18:13–23), he was able to reduce his workload by creating various positions that allowed other capable leaders to use their gifts and talents. A great leader recognizes and appreciates the giftedness of others, and shows this by releasing them into God's service.

Moses needed the gifts, talents, and natural abilities of other people to fulfill the will of God. And by reducing his workload, he was able to increase his leadership capacity. The right environment is one where the political, social, cultural, educational, economic, and religious structures are designed for leaders to resolve problems and remove barriers to creativity, innovation, and change.[3]

Christians, as God's moral agents, should harness creativity, innovation, and change into purposeful action and tackle the social ills that plague communities, societies, and the world. They can do this by developing leadership teams to research and organize programs that minister to the whole person. Possible areas of concentration include: (a) Feeding programs, (b) prison ministries, (c) hospital ministries, (d) nursing home ministries, (e) teen pregnancy ministries, (f) single parent ministries, and (g) drug and gang rehabilitation programs.

These are just a few areas where resources from organizations, institutions, businesses, and churches can be mobilized to triumph over human pain and suffering. The success of such efforts will be most measurable by the relationships established and the number of lives transformed from destructive behaviors or circumstances beyond their control. As new challenges arise in the world and unexpected events occur in the environment, good leaders will direct human resources, financial support, medical supplies, and natural resources to accommodate those needs.

To avoid potential pitfalls, leaders of organizations, institutions, businesses, and churches should create strategies and structures that foster good communication and collaboration.

Redefining environmental influences are only necessary when the environment has lost momentum, when it no longer meets the needs of its hurting, or when challenges bring more pressing issues to the forefront. Extreme environmental pressure is a clear indication that something needs to change, and the advice Moses received from his father-in-law, Jethro, illustrates this point.

Jethro had observed Moses and his leadership of Israel, and the fatigue in Moses' eyes and the sweat from his brow showed that his leadership style had some obvious flaws. Moses was exhausted because he was trying to settle every legal case the people brought to him, and the people were likewise weary because they waited so long for his judgment. With Jethro's help, Moses was able to devise a plan that allocated resources while maximizing performance.

In difficult situations, a leader must be assertive and decisive in defining problems and implementing solutions. You must realize that environmental problems require deliberate and decisive action that is driven by core values, communication, and collaboration. When you do these things, you will be less likely to micromanage processes, as Moses initially tried with Israel. You will be able to spend more time looking at the bigger picture and directing resources to meet needs in the most practical and efficient way, as Jethro's plan demonstrated.

It is a big challenge for a leader to step away from binding traditions when there are radical changes in the environment and the world. However, when leaders know who they are and what they want to accomplish, people are more inclined to volunteer their time, give of their resources, or host helpful events. Moses developed a process that resolved problems by using creativity and innovation. He organized Israel's institutional systems to enhance the effectiveness of their strategic formation.

STRATEGIC FORMATION AND IMPLEMENTATION

Strategic formation is a systematic discipline designed to provide a strategic plan for handling organizational and environmental issues. A successful strategic formation occurs when the entire organizational dynamic seeks to satisfy environmental concerns. The leader's compelling vision, strong mission, and core values translate into purposeful actions that benefit the organization, the environment, and the world.

Israel's strategic formation was designed to provide congruence between its strategies, structures, cultures, and processes. Jethro instructed Moses to develop a leadership team and to formulate a strategy with specific steps to help them resolve problems and minimize conflict. He said:

> Select capable men from all the people–men who fear God, trustworthy men who hate dishonest gain–and appoint them as officials over thousands, hundreds, fifties and tens. Have them serve as judges for the people at all times, but have them bring every difficult case to you; the simple cases they can decide themselves. That will make your load lighter, because they will share it with you. If you do this and God so commands, you will be able to stand the strain, and all these people will go home satisfied.
>
> —EXODUS 18:21–23

Strategic formation equipped Moses and his leadership team with the ability to adapt to changes while they maintained their focus. For Israel, what began as a method to resolve disputes in the wilderness slowly became an effective tool for establishing harmony and connectivity within groups. An organization must follow Israel's example, or it will fail.

Inefficient leadership is a clear indication of organizational and environmental misalignment. It points to a lack of congruency between an organization's strategic formation and its environmental pressures. To bring an organization back into alignment, you and your leadership team must design structures that reflect where your organization currently is and create strategies for where you want it to go. Finally, you must make the necessary changes to get there.

Strategizing and structuring around needs will bring an organization into alignment with its environment. It can then focus on the things it does best—serving the needs of others. Strategic formation involves five major areas:[4]

1. **Strategy**—A good strategy involves making decisions about who, what, when, where, and how the organization plans to operate in the environment.

2. **Structure**—Structuring involves goal-setting, clarifying expectations, efficiency, and continuity as a way to provide order.

3. **Culture**—Culture includes managing changes in the organization's dynamic and their effects upon the environment.

4. **Processes**—Good processes provide a clear sense of direction, energy, and empowerment to carry out the vision, mission, and values of the organization.

5. **Environmental Integration**—Integration involves ensuring that all systems perform as intended and are accepted and implemented.

The purpose of an organization's strategic formation is to keep the strategy, structure, culture, and process consistent with the environment. When this purpose is fulfilled, the organization and the environment are synchronized and benefit from the process. Failing to use the strategic formation approach may result in the following negative consequences: (a) Anomie, chaos, and purposelessness, (b) loss of synchronization, (c) loss of vision and opportunities, (d) misalignment of strategy, structure, the environment, and leadership.

Strategic formation can help an organization avoid mistakes that prevent it from reaching its goals. It is a process by which a leader can review what changes are needed and decide what impact they will have on the organization and its environment. Moses used strategic formation in Israel's organizational design because it worked.

THE IMPORTANCE OF
FAITH IN LEADERSHIP

T HE GENESIS OF faith in leadership predates the existence of humanity. The roots of faith can be found in the preexisting Supreme Being known as God, whose divine nature is depicted in the Creation account.

It was God who brought order to chaos and created a place for humanity to dwell. The biblical narrative gives the sense that God had a compelling vision of a beautiful garden that would be cared for and occupied by people with whom He would share fellowship on a continual basis. He began the creation process with no preexisting material. Genesis 1:1–3 says:

> In the beginning God created the heavens and the earth.
> Now the earth was formless and empty, darkness was
> over the surface of the deep, and the Spirit of God was
> hovering over the waters. And God said, "Let there be
> light," and there was light.

FAITH, THE DRIVING FORCE BEHIND CHANGE

The Genesis account supports the belief that creation was birthed from a desire driven by faith. Because the story reveals that God's words were followed by corresponding actions, God is in essence the originator of faith. A system of faith is inherent in Him, and He operates from it.

If the creation of humanity reveals that man is created in the image of God, a system of faith is also inherent within each person, waiting to be discovered (Rom. 12:3). Adam and Eve operated in faith to facilitate God's purposes. One of the most obvious examples of this was when God gave them a specific command not to eat of the tree of the knowledge of good and evil. Although they chose not to follow God's command, they had the capacity to obey Him. Underneath that capacity was a system of faith that became distorted as a result of sin.

God's faith compelled Him to rescue Adam and Eve. He did not allow them to live in a fallen state forever. Instead, moved with compassion for the human condition, He created a path for man to be restored. The restoration process finds it fullest expression in the redemptive work of Christ.

It is apparent that Jesus discovered the meaning of faith early in life because He knew at age twelve that God had called Him to a higher purpose. He was able to please the Father because His faith was properly aligned with the faith of His Father. As a leader, Jesus pleased God in every facet of His life. This was revealed when God declared, "You are my Son, whom I love; with you I am well pleased" (Mark 1:11).

Jesus' life and leadership was characterized by faith. His faith caused Him to heal the sick, cast out devils, raise the dead, and feed the multitudes with two pieces of fish and five loaves of bread (Luke 4:40–41; 7:14–15; 9:16). It also caused Him to embrace sinners, prostitutes, and the ill reputes of His day (Matt. 9:9–13, Luke 7:36–43). These acts of compassion were inherent in Jesus at birth, but He discovered them as He grew in faith and gained favor with God and man.

Jesus was the embodiment of faith that led to miraculous signs and wonders. He was a great motivating example for leaders to approach all of life with the eyes of faith. Jesus used God's Word to guide His decisions and shape His faith. Leaders must do the same.

The overriding objective of leadership is to seek and satisfy God's purposes in the earth. Leaders must strive to fulfill the biblical mandate and calling. They must learn to integrate their faith with their leadership to effect positive change around them. In essence, leadership is to be lived by faith in God.

When you are faced with difficult challenges or decisions, you must ask what Jesus would do. This helps you find the guidance and direction you need. Jesus never surrendered to adversity because He faced the most difficult challenges with the help of God.

LESSONS FROM THE STILLING OF THE STORM

The story of how Jesus stilled the storm (Mark 4:35–41) reminds leaders that they are dependent on God to guide them through difficult times. After a long day of teaching, Jesus proposed a trip across the Sea of Galilee. Because of the large crowd that sought after Him, it was impossible for Jesus to have a quiet moment to Himself, so He decided to leave the crowd behind. At His instruction, the disciples pointed their boat eastward toward the other side of the lake without a worry in sight.

Suddenly, a great storm, which was typical of the region, caught the fishermen by surprise. The Sea of Galilee was surrounded by hills, and this caused warm air to rise and cool air to rush down from the hills onto the lake. The result was a whirlwind action that churned the waters into an angry sea. The waves broke over the bow, filling the boat with water like a bathtub. Meanwhile, Jesus was sound asleep on a cushion in the stern of the boat.

Frightened, the disciples awoke Jesus and suggested that He was indifferent to their peril. Nothing could have been further from the truth. He got up and brought order out of chaos, showing His concern for His followers. Because Jesus had spent the majority of His time teaching His disciples about having faith in God, He thought that they would have been able to handle this difficulty. Scripture records that He rebuked the disciples for their lack of faith.

Jesus' demonstration of His sovereignty over both natural and supernatural elements awed the disciples and left them stunned at the way He handled difficult situations. As the Son of God, He exhibited His power over roaring elements. And through this particular lesson in natural leadership development, He showed how faith in leadership works to overcome chaotic situations.

Several principles of natural leadership development can be gleaned from this account. First, consider this phrase from Mark's narrative: "Let us go over to the other side" (Mark 4:35). The disciples often heard the words "let us go" during Jesus' ministry. His leadership was always on the move, and His compassion for the lost and hurting motivated Him to cross the political, social, and religious boundaries of His day.

Second, notice the phrase "leaving the crowd" (Mark 4:36). Although Jesus' ministry attracted the masses, He did not allow the people to draw Him away from His central mission. Likewise, leaders should not allow themselves to get caught up in the successes of their leadership only to lose sight of their mission.

The overarching mission for any leader is always to further God's purposes on earth. Jesus often preferred to leave the crowds to pray alone or to minister to small groups. This does not suggest that He preferred small groups over crowds. However, it does show that His mission remained the same regardless of the numbers. Success in leadership should not alter the original mission.

Third, although the storm caused the disciples to panic, Jesus was able to rest. His example shows that leaders must remain calm to weather the storms that threaten them. Resisting the urge to panic requires competency that comes from knowledge, skill, and experience. Jesus demonstrated that the strength of leadership lies within a leader's competency, integrity, and credibility. In the face of organizational and environmental disasters, leaders need faith to rest in the midst of the storm.

A fourth principle is that the disciples' cry for deliverance was answered. Jesus' stunning response to their plea demonstrates to leaders that He is able to calm the turbulence in our lives and in the world. Leaders are not required to know all or be all, but they are responsible to ask for help. Jesus did not need to calm the storm for His own sake, but He did it for the sake of those He loved. He is intimately involved in the affairs of leaders.

This knowledge alone can bring peace and tranquility to an otherwise difficult situation. Paul wrote the Philippians and said:

> The Lord is near. Do not be anxious about anything, but in everything, by prayer and petition, with thanksgiving, present your requests to God. And the peace of God, which transcends all understanding, will guard your hearts and your minds in Christ Jesus.
> —PHILIPPIANS 4:5–7

Finally, leaders must mirror the faith of Jesus if they are going to survive the turbulent waves of today's environment. During difficult times, it is helpful for leaders to surround themselves with wise, biblical counsel. Through the ministry of God's Word and the confirmation of the Holy Spirit, they can walk through storms in wholeness and integrity. Organizational and environmental activities must be guided by biblical principles if leaders are to avoid disastrous and costly mistakes.

FAITH: THE DETERMINANT OF PERSONAL AND ORGANIZATIONAL OUTCOMES

Personal and organizational outcomes are difficult to determine even with careful planning. But the best approach for measuring success is to measure the level of faith and commitment to personal and organizational goals. The Bible supports this, and its perspective of success is determined by two variables: faith and commitment. The apostle Paul revealed the true meaning of success when he wrote:

> I have fought the good fight, I have finished the race, I have kept the faith. Now there is in store for me the crown of righteousness, which the Lord, the righteous Judge, will award to me on that day—and not only to me, but also to all who have longed for his appearing.
> —2 TIMOTHY 4:7–8

It is impossible to accomplish anything without faith and commitment; they are the life and blood of success. Leaders must realize that the degree of success is equal to the degree of faith and commitment to the mission. Jesus' final declaration "It is finished" is the culmination of His faith and commitment to His mission, the salvation of humanity. In essence, what leaders give in terms of faith and commitment determines their level of success.

If the essence of leadership is influence, then the core of influence is relationships. If leaders do not learn how to have healthy relationships, they will ultimately have a negative impact on people, organizations, and the environment. Jesus taught by example that leadership at its core should be life-giving and life-sustaining. A good leader is one who possesses the mind of Christ, has the heart of a servant, is grieved by the lack of harmony, and seeks to bring wholeness to the interest of all.

The apostle Paul admonished leaders, as followers of Jesus, to adopt the attitude of Christ. He said:

> Your attitude should be the same as that of Christ Jesus: Who, being in very nature God, did not consider equality with God something to be grasped, but made himself nothing, taking the very nature of a servant, being made in human likeness. And being found in appearance as a man, he humbled himself and became obedient to death—even death on a cross!
>
> —PHILIPPIANS 2:5–8

Christians and many non-Christians esteem Jesus as the ultimate leader in history. Leaders ought to follow His example, for He is the express image of God. Consider Jesus' last words to His disciples, shortly before He faced His final hours:

> You call me "Teacher" and "Lord," and rightly so, for that is what I am. Now that I, your Lord and Teacher, have washed your feet, you also should wash one another's feet. I have set you an example that you should do as I have done for you.
>
> —JOHN 13:13–15

A good leader's life is characterized by a life of obedience to Christ—the fruit of faith—even as Jesus was obedient to the Father in all things.

6

POSTSCRIPT: PASSING THE
LEADERSHIP MANTLE

As stewards of God's grace, leaders must pass the lessons they have learned to the next generation; they can give no greater treasure. Leaving a legacy of greatness requires the passing of the leadership mantle, and this has become more important in today's changing environment.

Because of growing uncertainty in the marketplace, leaders are facing greater demands to develop transitional strategies for highly competent people to assume key leadership positions. The complexity of the economy and the competitive nature of the market are pushing leaders to the limit. All leaders shoulder the responsibilities of expanding the reach of their organizations by exploring new territories, finding new markets, and forging new relationships. Also, they must actively seek new insight, challenge old paradigms, and continually make the best of available resources.

All these factors are crucial to the survival of any organization or institution. But without a plan for replacing key leadership positions, companies will fold under the pressure to survive. Passing the reins of leadership to a new generation requires careful planning. If it is properly done, it will provide an avenue for achieving extraordinary results in the face of extraordinary change. However, it often fails because leaders lack insight about the impact the change will have on people.

Leaders must realize that this process requires letting go; this will enable them to take the first step toward finding the right replacement. Passing the leadership mantle provides an opportunity to bring people who are naturally gifted, talented, and skilled into the role of leadership. Qualified candidates will be flexible and adaptable to the changing environment. However, it would not be wise to consider candidates who revel in past success because they look back, instead of ahead, and often impede progress.

A social contract, a commitment between protégés and their mentors, is at the heart of any leadership transition. An individual's discipleship, loyalty, and consistent adherence to company policies are rewarded with increases in pay, responsibilities, and securities. Jesus upheld His contract with seventy-two of His disciples when He sent them out in Luke 10:1–24. He viewed His disciples' gifts, talents, skills, and natural abilities as an asset to the kingdom of God.

Most of the training provided to emerging leaders will not come from formal institutions, but from the environment. Hands-on leadership training provides opportunities for leaders to manage transitions, maximize performance, and reap the benefits of having a pool of highly skilled people from which to draw. Jesus used this method when He selected the twelve disciples:

> Jesus went up on a mountainside and called to him those he wanted, and they came to him. He appointed twelve—designating them apostles—that they might be

> with him and that he might send them out to preach and
> to have authority to drive out demons.
>
> —MARK 3:13–15

Jesus knew exactly what He was doing when He chose the twelve disciples. He considered not only their qualifications, but the deposit He would place in them. He knew that at God's appointed time, the seed of leadership He planted would eventually bear fruits of righteousness. Through this process, He would ultimately deliver people from the kingdom of darkness to the kingdom of light for generations to come. Christ's model of leadership training was no haphazard passing of the leadership mantle.

MANAGING LEADERSHIP TRANSITIONS

A successful passing of the leadership mantle does not just happen; it is largely determined by the choices leaders make about recruitment, training, advancement, replacement, and retirement. Failing to identify the necessary steps in finding key people is by far the greatest threat to any leadership in transition.

Passing the mantle requires an intimate knowledge of the potential leadership candidates. Note Jesus' comment to His disciple Nathanael:

> "Here is a true Israelite, in whom there is nothing false." "How do you know me?" Nathanael asked. Jesus answered, "I saw you while you were still under the fig tree before Philip called you." Then Nathanael declared, "Rabbi, you are the Son of God; you are the King of Israel."
>
> —JOHN 1:47–49

It is wise to invest the time necessary to become well acquainted with potential candidates. This will enable you to determine if the candidates are truly qualified to meet the challenges facing your organization.[1] A close relationship between you and your potential hire keeps both parties from having unrealistic expectations.[2]

To keep your focus on transitional planning and implementation, you must identify characteristics that potential candidates need to exemplify. You must also abandon the idea of finding the perfect replacement. R. Khurana says, "No single individual can save an organization."[3] This could be one reason why Jesus chose twelve disciples to continue His work on earth.

PASSING THE MANTLE: ELIJAH AND ELISHA

Passing the reins of leadership is one of the most difficult, yet fulfilling, aspects of natural leadership development. The difficulty lies in pouring one's knowledge, skills, and life experiences into another person. Most people initially resist being poured out like a drink offering, but a biblical understanding of leadership shows that this is necessary. Consider the expression of this principle in the narrative of the prophet Elijah's departure:

> So Elijah went from there and found Elisha son of Shaphat....Elijah went up to him and threw his cloak around him....Then he [Elisha] set out to follow Elijah and became his attendant.
> —1 KINGS 19:19–21

Toward the completion of his ministry, Elijah was charged with the task of anointing his successor, Elisha. This was a direct command from God, and it marked a permanent transition in the lives of these two men.

> The Lord said to him, "Go back the way you came, and go to the Desert of Damascus. When you get there, anoint

> Hazael king over Aram. Also, anoint Jehu son of Nimshi
> king over Israel, and anoint Elisha son of Shaphat from
> Abel Meholah to succeed you as prophet.
>
> —1 KINGS 19:15–16

Elijah had to face the harsh reality that his ministry was coming to a close. There is a bittersweet dimension to passing the leadership mantle. It is very difficult for a leader to release the reins of leadership that were held so diligently for many years. But no matter how hard it may be, every leader must face this reality.

To prepare for the transition, Elijah needed to allow ample time to develop a mentoring relationship with Elisha. A mentor as defined by Chip R. Bell in *Managers as Mentors* is "simply someone who helps someone else learn something the learner would otherwise have learned less well, more slowly, or not at all."[4]

To walk in the full measure of his leadership anointing, Elisha had to embrace his new role as Elijah's protégé. He had to be willing to leave his familiar surroundings and accept the challenges ahead of him. He also had to be willing to humble himself like a child and receive Elijah's instructions. A lack of humility on Elisha's part would have made it difficult for Elijah to teach and coach him. He would not have been able to enjoy the benefits of Elijah's natural leadership development lessons.

This principle is important: A lack of humility on the part of any protégé is a clear indication that he or she is not ready for leadership responsibilities. An emerging leader must be able to follow before being able to lead. The fieldwork, or grunt work, prepared Elisha to assume his new role and responsibilities. Elisha's humility allowed him to reap the benefits of Elijah's knowledge, skills, and experiences, which ultimately enabled him to do twice as much as his predecessor.

CHARACTERISTICS
OF A SUCCESSFUL TRANSITION

Because transitional relationships are designed for the future leader's growth, mentoring should always be evaluated to ensure the best training possible. The mentor should assess strengths and weaknesses and seek ways to improve the quality of materials and maintain a standard of excellence. Success or failure will show how well the passing of leadership responsibilities has been executed.

A commitment to natural leadership development will create a spirit that is dedicated to life and learning. The strategy is simple: (a) Get others involved in the process; (b) see to it that leaders facilitate the learning process; (c) keep the vision, mission, and message alive by passing them on.

Mentoring relationships typically end once the protégé has gained a sufficient amount of information to achieve the overall objective. Elijah's and Elisha's mentoring relationship continued to grow until Elijah was taken up in a whirlwind. But just before his celebrated departure he passed his mantle to Elisha:

> And Elijah went up by a whirlwind into heaven. And Elisha saw it, and he cried out, "My father, my father, the chariot of Israel and its horsemen!" So he saw him no more…He also took up the mantle of Elijah…,"
>
> —2 KINGS 2:11–13, NKJV

The mentoring relationship of Elijah and Elisha was similar to that of Jesus and His disciples. Jesus groomed His disciples for leadership, and the body of Christ has enjoyed the fruits of their dynamic relationship ever since.

61

MENTORING RELATIONSHIPS:
THE KEY TO A LASTING LEGACY

The mentoring relationship is the most profound element in the natural leadership development process. The most powerful contribution a leader can make in the life of a protégé is to help him become a leader. Leaders produce leaders. Christ invested His life in His followers and produced leaders. Out of a deep sense of servitude for God, Christ was able to bring healing to the sick, water to the thirsty, food to the hungry, and life to the dead. He passed His vision, mission, message, and methods to His disciples.

Great leaders leave a legacy of greatness for others to follow. They not only set the bar for others, but they help others reach and exceed their limits by depositing in them the valuable lessons they have learned. Generally, mentors and their protégés should meet on a regular basis to share their dreams, business philosophies, and new ideas. A healthy aspect of any strategic endeavor allows time for reflection, meditation, contemplation, and transformation. This keeps leaders and their protégés highly focused and energized.

With all the changes and staggering increases in leadership complexities, leaders must give more consideration to the preparation of others. To do otherwise would be a disastrous mistake. Leaders learn the majority of their knowledge from others. Truly great leaders commit their time and resources to the development of others so that their vision and mission will live on through future generations.

ABOUT THE AUTHOR

M cKinley Johnson is the founder and pastor of Eternal Life Church. As a California native, McKinley had the awesome privilege of making the principal's honor roll, earning him the honor of being listed in *Who's Who Among America's High School Students*. Like so many other students McKinley learned to overcome adversity early on. He didn't allow hardships and disappointments to stand in the way of pursuing his dreams.

McKinley was encouraged to pursue with great vigor God's plan and purpose for his life. His parents believed that in order for him to achieve his personal, academic, and professional goals they had to be actively involved. The discipline and hard work his parents taught him helped him to obtain an honorable discharge from the United States Navy. Among his many accomplishments are the following scholastic degrees:

- ◆ Associate in Arts (Compton College, Compton, California)

- Bachelor of Arts in Ministry and Leadership (Vanguard University, Costa Mesa, California)

- Master of Business Administration (Azusa Pacific University, Azusa, California)

- Certificate of Advanced Graduate Studies in Organizational Leadership (Regent University, Virginia Beach, Virginia)

- Doctor of Strategic Leadership (Regent University, Virginia Beach, Virginia)

These various accomplishments are a vital part of God's strategic plan for his life and ministry. Dr. Johnson teaches that God sometimes gives us a vision, which we find both fascinating and frightening. He did just that to him when in January 1995 He planted the idea in his mind to start a local church. The vision is still unfolding, but the birth of the church was realized in August 1995.

BIBLIOGRAPHY

Bell, C. R. *Managers as Mentors*. San Francisco: Berrett-Koehler Publishers, 1998.

Bell, W. *Foundations of Futures Studies: History, Purposes, and Knowledge*, vol. 1. New Brunswick, NJ: Transaction Publishers, 2003.

Bishop, P. *Applied Futurism: An Emerging Discipline*. (Tech. Rep.). Houston, TX: University of Houston-Clear Lake, 1997.

Bridges, W. *Managing Transitions: Making the Most of Change*. Reading, MA: Addison-Wesley, 1991.

Buzzell, S., K. Boa, and B. Perkins. *The Leadership Bible: Leadership Principles From God's Word*. Grand Rapids, MI: Zondervan Publishing House, 1998.

Ciulla, J.B. *Ethics: the Heart of Leadership*. Westport, CT: Praeger, 1998.

Daft, R. *Leadership Theory and Practice*. Orlando, FL: The Dryden Press, 1999.

Daft, R. *Organization Theory and Design*, seventh edition. Cincinnati, OH: South-Western College Publishing, 2001.

Depree, M. *Leadership Is An Art*. New York: Dell Publishing, 1989.

Grenier, R. and G. Metes. *Going Virtual: Moving Your Organization Into The 21st Century*. Upper Saddle River, NJ: Prentice Hall, 1995.

Gryskiewics, S. *Positive Turbulence: Developing Climates for Creativity, Innovation, and Renewal*. San Francisco: Jossey-Bass Publishers, 1999.

Joas, Hans. *The Genesis of Values*. Chicago, IL: University of Chicago Press, 2000.

Khurana, R. *Searching for a Corporate Savior: The Irrational Quest for Charismatic CEOs*. Princeton, NJ: Princeton University Press, 2002.

Malphurs, A. *Values-Driven Leadership: Discovering and Developing Your Core Values for Ministry*. Grand Rapids, MI: Baker Books, 1996.

Nelson, D. and J. Quick. *Organizational Behavior: The Essentials.* St. Paul, MN: West Publishing Company, 1996.

Newbigin, L. *The Gospel in a Pluralist Society.* Grand Rapids, MI: Wm. B. Eerdmans Publishing Co., 1989.

Ringland, G. *Scenario Planning: Managing for the Future.* New York: John Wiley & Sons, 1998.

Rokeach, M. *Understanding Human Values: Individual and Societal.* New York: The Free Press, 1979.

Rothwell, W. J. *Effective Succession Planning: Ensuring Leadership Continuity and Building Talent From Within,* second edition. New York: American Management Association, 2001.

Sargent, M. "The Real Scandal: Enron's Crimes Were Legal." *Commonwealth,* March 2002, 10.

Snyder, H. *The Community of the King.* Downers Grove, IL: Inter-Varsity Press, 1977.

Wren, D. A. *The Evolution of Management Thought,* fourth edition. New York, NY: John Wiley & Sons, 1994.

Yukl, G. *Leadership in Organizations,* fifth edition. Upper Saddle River, NJ: Prentice-Hall, 2002.

SUGGESTED READING

♦ Ashkenas, R., D. Ulrich, T. Jick, and S. Kerr, *The Boundaryless Organization: Breaking the Chains of Organizational Structure.* San Francisco: Jossey-Bass, 2002.

♦ Boundon, R. *The Origin of Values: Sociology and Philosophy of Beliefs.* New Brunswick, NJ: Transaction Publishers, 2001.

♦ Chewning, R., J. Eby, and S. Roels. *Business Through the Eyes of Faith.* New York: HarperCollins Publisher, 1990.

♦ Gary, J. *The Future According to Jesus.* Paper presented at Regent University for DSL Residency, Virginia Beach, VA, September 18, 2003.

♦ Hitt, M., R. Ireland, and R. Hoskisson. *Strategic Management: Competitiveness and Globalization,* third edition. Cincinnati, OH: South-Western College Publishing, 1999.

♦ Hoyle, J. *Leadership and Futuring: Making Visions Happen.* Thousand Oaks, CA: Corwin Press, 1995.

♦ Kuczmarski, S. and T. Kuczmarski. *Values-Based Leadership: Rebuilding Employee Commitment, Performance, & Productivity.* New Jersey, NJ: Prentice Hall, 1995.

- McCall, M. Jr. and G. Hollenbeck. *Developing Global Executives: The Lessons of International Experience.* Boston: Harvard Business School Press, 2002.

- Mintzberg, H., B. Ahlstrand, and J. Lampel. *Strategy Safari: A Guided Tour Through the Wilds of Strategic Management.* New York: The Free Press, 1998.

- Schaller, L. *Strategies for Change.* Nashville, TN: Abingdon Press, 1993.

- Senge, P. *The Fifth Discipline: The Art & Practice of the Learning Organization.* New York: Dell Publishing, 1990.

NOTES

Introduction

1. G. Yukl, *Leadership in Organizations*, fifth edition (Upper Saddle River, NJ: Prentice-Hall, 2002).

CHAPTER 1:
Biblical Roots of Natural Leadership Development

1. M. Depree, *Leadership Is an Art* (New York: Dell Publishing, 1989).
2. S. Buzzell, K. Boa, and B. Perkins, *The Leadership Bible: Leadership Principles From God's Word* (Grand Rapids, MI: Zondervan Publishing House, 1973, 1998).
3. Ray Grenier and George Metes, *Going Virtual: Moving Your Organization Into the 21st Century* (Upper Saddle River, NJ: Prentice Hall, 1995).
4. S. Gryskiewics, *Positive Turbulence: Developing Climates for Creativity, Innovation, and Renewal* (San Francisco: Jossey-Bass Publishers, 1999).

CHAPTER 2:
God-Initiated Leadership

1. M. Sargent, "The Real Scandal: Enron's Crimes Were Legal," *Commonwealth*, *129*(5), March 8, 2002, 10.
2. Milton Rokeach, *Understanding Human Values: Individual and Societal* (New York: The Free Press, 1979).
3. Hans Joas, *The Genesis of Values* (Chicago, IL: University of Chicago Press, 2000).
4. A. Malphurs, *Values-Driven Leadership: Discovering and Developing Your Core Values for Ministry* (Grand Rapids, MI: Baker Books, 1996).

5. Joanne B. Ciulla, *Ethics the Heart of Leadership* (Westport, CT: Praeger, 1998).
6. Ibid.
7. Malphurs, *Values-Driven Leadership: Discovering and Developing Your Core Values for Ministry.*

CHAPTER 3:
The Seed of Leadership and Its Healing Impact

1. L. Newbigin, *The Gospel in a Pluralist Society* (Grand Rapids, MI: Wm. B. Eerdmans Publishing Co., 1989).
2. G. Yukl, *Leadership in Organizations*, fifth edition (Upper Saddle River, NJ: Prentice-Hall, 2002).
3. Ibid.
4. R. Daft, *Leadership Theory and Practice* (Orlando, FL: The Dryden Press, 1999).
5. D. Nelson, and J. Quick, *Organizational Behavior: The Essentials* (St. Paul, MN: West Publishing Company, 1996).
6. Ibid.
7. P. Bishop, *Applied Futurism: An Emerging Discipline*, Tech. Rep. (Houston, TX: University of Houston-Clear Lake, 1997).
8. G. Ringland, *Scenario Planning: Managing for the Future* (New York: John Wiley & Sons, 1998).
9. W. Bell, *Foundations of Futures Studies: History, Purposes, and Knowledge*, vol. 1 (New Brunswick, NJ: Transaction Publishers, 2003).
10. S. Buzzell, K. Boa, and B. Perkins, *The Leadership Bible: Leadership Principles From God's Word* (Grand Rapids, MI: Zondervan Publishing House, 1973, 1998).
11. Howard A. Snyder, *The Community of the King* (Downers Grove, IL: Inter-Varsity Press, 1977).

CHAPTER 4:
Recognizing the Environment for All Its Worth

1. D. A. Wren, *The Evolution of Management Thought*, fourth edition (New York, NY: John Wiley & Sons, 1994).
2. R. Daft, *Organization Theory and Design*, seventh edition (Cincinnati, OH: South-Western College Publishing, 2001).

3. Ibid.
4. R. Daft, *Leadership Theory and Practice* (Orlando, FL: The Dryden Press, 1999).

CHAPTER 5:
The Importance of Faith in Leadership

1. W. Bridges, *Managing Transitions: Making the Most of Change* (Reading, MA: Addison-Wesley, 1991).

CHAPTER 6:
Postscript: Passing the Leadership Mantle

1. W.J. Rothwell, *Effective Succession Planning: Ensuring Leadership Continuity and Building Talent From Within*, second edition (New York: American Management Association, 2001).
2. R. Khurana, *Searching for a Corporate Savior: The Irrational Quest for Charismatic CEOs* (Princeton, NJ: Princeton University Press, 2002).
3. Ibid.
4. Chip R. Bell, *Managers as Mentors* (San Francisco: Berrett-Koehler Publishers, 1998).